# SALES MADE SIMPLE

Based on *More Sales Please* by Sara Nasser Dalrymple

First published in Great Britain by Practical Inspiration Publishing, 2025

© Sara Nasser Dalrymple and Practical Inspiration Publishing, 2025

The moral rights of the author have been asserted.

ISBN  978-1-78860-753-7  (paperback)
      978-1-78860-754-4  (epub)
      978-1-78860-755-1  (Kindle)

All rights reserved. This book, or any portion thereof, may not be reproduced without the express written permission of the publisher.

Every effort has been made to trace copyright holders and to obtain their permission for the use of copyright material. The publisher apologizes for any errors or omissions and would be grateful if notified of any corrections that should be incorporated in future reprints or editions of this book.

EU GPSR representative: LOGOS EUROPE, 9 rue Nicolas Poussin, LA ROCHELLE 17000, France Contact@logoseurope.eu

Want to bulk-buy copies of this book for your team and colleagues? We can customize the content and co-brand *Sales Made Simple* to suit your business's needs.

Please email info@practicalinspiration.com for more details.

# Contents

Series introduction ............................................................. iv

Introduction ........................................................................ 1

Day 1: We are all salespeople now ................................ 5

Day 2: Ditching the myths .............................................. 13

Day 3: Diagnose your sales problem ......................... 23

Day 4: The ten non-negotiables of selling well ...... 33

Day 5: The buyer journey ............................................... 41

Day 6: Solid sales foundations ..................................... 49

Day 7: Sales strategy step by step .............................. 60

Day 8: The power of your personal brand ............... 72

Day 9: Turning your content into sales .................... 83

Day 10: Take the 30-day sales challenge ................. 94

Conclusion ....................................................................... 105

Endnotes .......................................................................... 108

# Series introduction

Welcome to *6-Minute Smarts*!

This is a series of very short books with one simple purpose: to introduce you to ideas that can make life and work better, and to give you time and space to think about how those ideas might apply to your life and work.

Each book introduces you to ten powerful ideas, but ideas on their own are useless – that's why each idea is followed by self-coaching questions to help you work out the 'so what?' for you in just six minutes of exploratory writing. What's exploratory writing? It's the kind of writing you do just for yourself, fast and free, without worrying what anyone else thinks. It's not just about getting ideas out of your head and onto paper where you can see them, it's about finding new connections and insights as you write. This is where the magic happens.

Find out more...

# Introduction

If you're ready to simplify the way you make money, increase sales with ease and grow your business without the grind, you're going to love this book. There are lots of people who'll try to convince you that making a success of your business is very, very complicated. I'm not one of them.

There's a common belief that exists in the small business community, that it's impossible to market yourself online without coming across as sleazy or icky. I think this one sneaky limiting belief is responsible for millions of pounds in lost revenue every week. So I decided to write this guide to help creatives, small business owners and first-time entrepreneurs sell without the sleaze.

In a recent poll of 1,000 small businesses in the UK, over 90% said they felt invisible online and 60% said they don't use social media at all.[1] The businesses making the most money are the ones that understand the importance of showing up in small, repeatable ways to meet their audience where they're at. It's not about trying to 'get the sale' any more. Now, the most important job you have is to make it easy for people to make aligned decisions on their own timeline.

The way we choose how and where to spend our money has changed forever as a result of the internet-based devices we all carry around in our hands. Buyers today like to look online to aid the decision-making process of figuring out what to buy and who to buy it from. Whether that's a website, social media platform or emails, your buyers are pretty savvy. They know exactly what they want, and they can come online whenever they fancy to find it.

Your clients are busy. They are living hectic lives, bombarded with millions of marketing messages and decisions to make every single day. The single best gift you can give them is the gift of ease. The person who makes it the easiest wins the sale.

That levels off the playing field and gives the small business community a *huge* opportunity – one that we've never ever had before. We are no longer competing against big companies with big budgets, big advertising campaigns and big teams. We now get to make as many sales as we want, just with clear

## Introduction

messaging, a commitment to good service and the phones in our hands.

If you run a business, or want to, it has never been easier for you to be found by a steady stream of ideal buyers. We are living in a time when, for the first time ever, we can be business owners, choose our hours and work in a way that supports ourselves, our well-being, our available time and the life we want to lead. I think that's pretty cool, and I won't have it squandered because of an outdated stereotype about how to sell things. And you can start right away! You don't need a huge audience and you don't need to be an expert on social media – all you need is this book and a few minutes each day.

Here you'll find ten tasks to simplify your sales so that you can keep your business in funds, make more money and grow without the grind. You'll gain more clarity, more confidence and more ease. And by the time you've finished, you'll know exactly what you need to do to make more sales in your business.

You're in the right place if:

- You want the way you sell to be simple, effective and 100% sleaze-free
- You're fed up of guessing at how to attract a steady stream of sales and you want a step-by-step process to follow

- You'd like any time you spend online to convert to actual sales
- You're ready to understand how to meet your clients online with the exact information they need to help them decide to buy from you again and again, recommend you to all their friends and become loyal fans of what you do
- You don't feel like a confident sales person and you know it's holding you back
- You love the idea of having less actions on your to-do list and more money in your bank account

Every chapter is packed with time-saving prompts and actions you can take in just a few minutes each day. If every business owner out there spent just 30 minutes a day talking about what they do, millions would be generated every week. I want you to work in a way that is spacious and energizing and where burn-out isn't the cost of being successful. I don't for one second believe work should be all-consuming. We all get to have a business that supports ease. To stop struggling. To be paid properly. And to finally get off the grind for good.

Let's go!

# Day 1
# We are all salespeople now

When I first started promoting my business on social media, it felt like I'd landed on Mars. I knew how to sell and market in the 'real' world, but suddenly I was a complete newbie. Instagram, which I had always used as a photo-sharing app, became something else entirely – a potential sales tool. And the step-up felt enormous. It was like being in a new job where you don't even know where the loos are and you spend all day trying to fit in.

There seemed to be a whole new set of rules for online business and a new language to learn, filled with words like 'algorithm', 'discovery calls', 'memes' and 'hashtags'. It was overwhelming. Everywhere I turned, I found a new opinion about what you had to do to find clients online:

- 'You need to grow your audience to 10,000 followers first!'
- 'You need a lead magnet!'
- 'You need to be known for one clear niche!'
- 'You need a Facebook group!'
- 'You need to go live every day!'
- 'You need to handle objections!'

It felt like a lot to navigate. The internet was awash with 'guru' coaches claiming to have the perfect system for online sales, offering quick fixes, fancy hacks and must-have scripts. Eager to get it right, I rolled up my sleeves and immersed myself in learning.

This might sound odd given my background in corporate sales. Surely I already knew how to sell, right? But as a new business owner, I didn't want to take a wrong turn. I wanted to follow the 'rules' for online selling, if they existed, and avoid wasting time on strategies that didn't work.

## What selling really means

Selling is not about convincing, pressuring or manipulating anyone. It's about providing clarity and creating an easy decision-making process for your clients. When you do this consistently, selling becomes an extension of your values – it feels effortless, aligned and even enjoyable.

If sales are the lifeblood of your business, then sales skills are the foundation on which it's built. These skills ensure you can:

- Make money from day one
- Build a sustainable business
- Work efficiently, without draining all your time
- Help your clients make decisions with confidence and ease

A business without strong sales skills is like a house built on mud. It might look fine from the outside, but without a solid foundation, it won't hold up in the long run.

## Marketing and selling: two sides of the same coin

It's important to understand the difference between marketing and selling, especially when you're running a small business.

Marketing is about raising awareness. It's how you introduce your business to potential clients, share your story and let people know what you do. Selling, on the other hand, is about guiding those potential clients through the decision-making process.

In big corporations, marketing and sales are often handled by separate teams. But as a small business owner, you wear both hats. Marketing and selling work hand in hand: one builds connections, and the other helps convert those connections into sales. If you only focus on marketing, you risk creating great content that never leads to sales. If you only focus on selling, you miss the opportunity to build trust and long-term relationships.

Your sales process combines both marketing and selling into a clear, intentional path for your clients. It's a series of actions that help potential buyers move from curiosity to clarity, equipping them to make empowered decisions. This process is unique to your business, shaped by your preferences, personality and the clients you want to attract.

## The power of a great sales experience

As small business owners, we have a unique advantage: we can create deeply personal, memorable experiences for our clients. Unlike big companies, where clients are passed from one department to another, we have the ability to provide consistency and care at every stage of the buying journey.

A great sales experience isn't just about making a transaction. It's about making your client feel seen, heard and understood. When you prioritize the client experience, you set yourself apart as someone who genuinely cares. And that creates loyalty, repeat business and glowing referrals.

Think about the best sales experience you've ever had. What made it stand out? Was it the way you were spoken to? The clarity of the process? The feeling that your needs were genuinely understood?

Now think about the worst sales experience you've had. What went wrong? Was it the lack of clarity? The feeling of being ignored? Or something else?

Use these experiences as a guide to shape how you sell in your business. Decide what kind of experience you want to create for your clients, whether they're brand new or returning for the tenth time.

## Feel-good selling

Selling doesn't have to feel awkward or uncomfortable. When you focus on the overall experience your clients have, selling becomes a natural extension of your commitment to serve them.

This shift in mindset – from 'How do I sell?' to 'How can I create a great experience?' – is small but powerful. It takes the pressure off you and puts the focus where it belongs: on helping your clients make decisions that feel right for them.

Sales is an exchange of energy. When you genuinely love what you're selling, your enthusiasm is contagious. And when your clients feel excited and cared for, they'll buy not just once but again and again.

 So what? Over to you...

1. Think of a really great sales experience you've had. What made it stand out? What did you like about it? How did you feel?

2. Now, think of a less positive one. What was it about this experience that didn't feel good?

3. Sales is an energy exchange. Using your brainstorms from above, set your intention: how do you want clients to feel when they decide to buy from you?

# Day 2
# Ditching the myths

Have you ever felt like you're the only business owner who isn't selling out programmes, growing at lightning speed or setting off celebratory confetti cannons on social media? When you're working tirelessly to grow your business but not seeing the traction you'd like, it can feel exhausting, frustrating and demoralizing.

The truth is that for most people, growing a sustainable business takes time, patience, planning and perseverance. If you're looking for a quick-fix, one-size-fits-all strategy for building a million-pound business in two minutes flat, this isn't the book for you.

Instead, I'm here to help you sell in a way that feels natural, effortless and aligned with your personality, values and stage of business. Let's start by addressing the elephant in the room: the substandard, sleazy sales practices that give selling a bad name.

## Why do sales get such a bad rap?

If you've ever been on the receiving end of a pushy or manipulative sales experience, you're not alone. Some common examples include:

- Coaches promising one-on-one support who disappear after you invest
- Scarcity tactics – like time-sensitive bonuses – that never materialize
- Salespeople who don't bother to learn your name, let alone understand your needs

These experiences reinforce harmful stereotypes: that salespeople are greedy, pushy or self-serving. While these behaviours exist, they're not representative of the caring, creative and community-driven small business owners I work with every day.

The world needs more integrity-led sellers. Unfortunately, many small business owners are so afraid of being pushy that they avoid selling altogether, even working for free or at rates that don't

## Ditching the myths

cover their bills. Fear around selling is costly – not just for individuals but for the economy as a whole.

## Sales myths and the truths to replace them

The fear and hesitation many feel about selling often stem from outdated myths. Let's tackle some of the most persistent ones.

## Myth 1: Selling is sleazy, manipulative or pushy

This myth suggests that selling is about tricking people into buying something they don't need. Everyone has encountered the stereotypical pushy salesperson: the door-to-door rep with slippery tactics, the fitness professional shaming you into action or the used-car dealer who just wants to close the deal.

**Truth:** Selling, at its core, is about helping people make informed decisions. By connecting on a human level, building relationships, and offering clear information, you can sell with integrity – no sleaze required.

## Myth 2: You need a big audience to make sales online

Scrolling through social media, it's easy to believe that success requires a massive following. If sales aren't coming in, it's tempting to think the problem is your audience size rather than your sales strategy.

**Truth:** A big audience doesn't guarantee sales. If you're not making sales with the audience you have, the solution isn't to grow it – it's to learn how to sell effectively to your existing audience. Focus on creating a sales plan and showing up consistently.

Many business owners put off selling because they believe they need a larger audience. This is self-sabotage. If you're not actively working on your sales skills, it won't matter how many followers you have. Start selling from day one and grow your audience as you go.

## Myth 3: Sales is purely transactional

Some selling styles focus entirely on one-off transactions, with no emphasis on relationships or repeat business. This approach might work for big businesses with endless streams of customers, but it's not effective for small, heart-led businesses.

*Ditching the myths*

**Truth:** As a small business owner, you're selling more than a product or service – you're selling an experience. Building relationships and offering personal touches lead to repeat business, referrals and glowing reviews. Selling isn't just about the sale – it's about creating a lasting connection.

## Myth 4: The best salespeople are loud extroverts

Many people assume that selling requires a big, bold personality. If you're naturally quieter or more introverted, you might feel like you're not cut out for sales.

**Truth:** The best salespeople aren't the loudest – they're the ones who listen. Understanding your client's needs and responding thoughtfully is far more important than dominating the conversation. Selling isn't about being someone you're not – it's about showing up authentically.

## Myth 5: Good products sell themselves

It's easy to believe that if your product isn't selling, there must be something wrong with it. And some creatives may avoid the discomfort of selling by assuming their work should 'speak for itself'.

**Truth:** Even the best products need visibility. If people don't know about your product, or don't understand how it can help them, they won't buy it. Selling isn't about pushing people – it's about helping them discover the value of what you offer.

## Rewriting the narrative around selling

It's time to ditch these myths and replace them with a new truth: selling is how you serve your clients. The more confident you become at selling, the more people you can help and the more your business can thrive.

Selling isn't about using outdated, ill-fitting tactics borrowed from big business boardrooms. You don't have to rely on scripts, pressure or flashy gimmicks. Instead, you get to create a sales process that's personal, human and values-driven. And one that shares useful information.

Here's a quick truth to take forward: 'My clients don't want to be sold to – they want to be informed.'

- Your clients want genuine interaction, not scripts.
- They want human connection, not to feel like a number.

*Ditching the myths*

- They want an experience that goes beyond a transaction.

Selling with integrity means showing up as yourself, building relationships and offering solutions. It's not about persuading – it's about positioning. By helping your clients make decisions aligned with their goals, you're creating a sales experience they'll want to repeat.

## Build your sales confidence

To rewrite your own narrative around selling, start by reflecting on your experiences as a buyer.

- What has made the best sales experiences stand out for you?
- What turned you off in negative sales encounters?

Use these insights to shape how you sell in your business. Decide what kind of experience you want your clients to have – then commit to creating it consistently.

So what? Over to you…

1. Taking stereotypes into account, which is holding you back the most?

## Ditching the myths

2. Create a new sales truth. Write down at least five good things that will happen when you feel confident at selling.

3. From the list, which is your favourite? Affirm it to yourself every day. Where can you write this new belief so that you see it each morning?

# Day 3
# Diagnose your sales problem

When I launched my very first product online, it completely flopped. Not one person bought it.

If there's anything more disheartening than pouring your heart and soul into something only to finally release it to the world and the response to be... nothing, then I don't what it is. At the time, it felt crushing. Looking back, I can see exactly why it happened: my messaging was vague. I was a wedding photographer marketing myself as a 'natural wedding photographer'. But what did that even mean? It wasn't clear, and it certainly wasn't compelling.

The lesson here? The best way to learn what works is to take action, even messy action, and adjust as you go. Every business owner I know has had flops. The key is to keep going and figure out what needs to change. Now, every course, programme and product I launch sells well. And I'm going to show you how to fast-track your success.

If your sales aren't flowing the way you'd like, there's likely a specific problem holding you back. Let's get to the bottom of what that problem is so you can take action with clarity and confidence.

## Common sales problems and how to solve them

### Problem 1: You're an over-deliverer

If you're constantly giving away free advice but holding back when it comes to promoting your paid products, you might be over-delivering.

### What it looks like

- You focus on providing solutions through free content, hoping it will inspire people to buy from you.
- You regularly share tips and resources but avoid directly talking about your services or products.

## The issue

Your content is heavily weighted toward free value, but it's not helping your audience make decisions. While your tips are helpful, they can overwhelm rather than encourage action. Without clear guidance on how to progress from free content to paid services, your audience remains stuck.

## The solution

Shift your focus to creating content that spells out who your products are for, what they offer and how they work. Highlight the transformation your services provide and the results clients can expect. This approach empowers your audience to make confident decisions about working with you.

# Problem 2: You're a sales-phobe (not selling enough)

If the idea of selling feels uncomfortable or even terrifying, you might be a sales-phobe.

## What it looks like

- You avoid promoting your products because you don't want to seem pushy.
- You focus on perfecting your products and hope they'll sell themselves.

## The issue

You're waiting for clients to find you on their own, but your lack of visibility is slowing your progress. Without actively showing up and sharing your message, your audience doesn't have the information they need to decide if your services are right for them.

## The solution

You are the face of your business. Sharing your story and showing up consistently is what builds trust and connection. Start small. Instead of thinking, 'I need to sell today', try asking, 'How can I show up for my audience in a way that feels good?' The more visible you are, the more clarity you provide – and the more confident your audience will feel about buying from you.

## Problem 3: You're a sales enthusiast

If you're actively promoting your services but not seeing consistent results, you might be a sales enthusiast with a transactional approach.

### What it looks like

- You regularly talk about your products and services.
- You've had some success but find that many sales conversations don't convert.

### The issue

Your content is too focused on the sale itself, with little attention to building personal connections. Without creating curiosity or demand, your audience may feel disengaged or uninspired.

### The solution

Balance your content by sharing more about the people your services are designed for, the results they can expect and the process of working with you. Connection and curiosity are essential for building demand. By warming up your audience with this type of content, you'll make it easier for them to move from interest to action.

## Problem 4: You're a flip-flopper (selling at random)

If your sales efforts are inconsistent, you might be a flip-flopper.

### What it looks like

- You promote your services in bursts, depending on your energy or inspiration.
- You don't follow a clear sales plan, which leads to gaps in your visibility.

### The issue

Without a consistent strategy, it's hard to build momentum. Sporadic promotions can feel jarring to your audience, making it harder for them to trust or engage with your message.

### The solution

Commit to simple, repeatable actions. Even 10–15 minutes a day of focused sales activity can have a big impact over time. Repeating key messages regularly helps your audience understand what you offer and why it's right for them.

## Diagnosing your sales problem

Identifying your specific sales problem is the first step to improving your results. Once you know where the issue lies, you can focus on the actions that will make the biggest difference for you.

- **If you're an over-deliverer:** Focus on showcasing your products and making it clear who they're for.
- **If you're a sales-phobe:** Start taking small steps to make yourself more visible.
- **If you're a sales enthusiast:** Rebalance your content to include more connection-building.
- **If you're a flip-flopper:** Commit to consistent, repeatable sales actions.

The right sales activity depends on where you are now. By focusing on intentional, strategic action, you'll create the momentum needed to grow your business.

## So what? Over to you…

1. Take the quiz on my website to discover your biggest sales problem (and what to do about it) – you can find this at: https://saradalrymple.co.uk/quiz.

## Diagnose your sales problem

2. Look at the report with your results: what one action can you take today to help you resolve your key sales problem?

3. Set aside 30 minutes a day to focus on your sales, and block that time in your calendar so it definitely happens. How will you protect that time?

# Day 4
# The ten non-negotiables of selling well

After the Covid-19 pandemic, I experienced burn-out first hand. Home-schooling two young children alongside running a home and a business took its toll. It took me a year to recover. After this experience, I realized two things: (1) Your energy is a precious business asset and (2) I needed to make a change.

## Burn-out and the business owner

Burn-out is a widespread issue among business owners. Balancing income uncertainty, decision fatigue and domestic responsibilities – often without a team to lean on – can be overwhelming. If left unchecked, your business can consume all your time and energy, even before you hit profitability.

As we've already discovered, selling is an exchange of energy: you share your passion and enthusiasm for what you do, and that energy resonates with your audience. But when burn-out strikes, your capacity to connect disappears. Dragging yourself through the motions of promoting your business is both exhausting and ineffective.

After my own experience with burn-out, I had to make a change. I simplified the way I worked and shifted to a lighter, more efficient way of selling. Instead of relying on complex strategies, I focused on clear, repeatable actions I could take in just a few minutes each day. It worked – and it's a strategy I'll never abandon.

## Everyday selling: the needle movers

Everyday selling isn't about doing everything – it's about prioritizing the right things to ensure your business stays in funds. It's knowing the difference between activities that drive sales and those that don't, and focusing your energy on what truly matters. Here are the ten non-negotiable tasks that will help you sell well:

## *The ten non-negotiables of selling well*

### 1. Create an experience you love

Selling is easier – and more effective – when you love what you're offering. If you're not obsessed with your product or service, how can you expect your audience to be? Passion is contagious, so make sure your offers light you up.

### 2. Sell to the audience you have

You don't need a massive audience to make sales. Start by selling to the people already in your community. The better you become at connecting with your first ten clients, the easier it will be to scale later.

### 3. Remove the guesswork

Guessing wastes time and drains energy. Instead, diagnose your sales problem, set clear goals and create a plan of action. A clear strategy will save you time and get you noticed by the right clients.

### 4. Know your needle movers

Focus your energy on the tasks that truly matter – these are your needle movers. Prioritize actions that directly contribute to sales and client relationships, and let go of distractions that don't serve your business.

## 5. Be easy to buy from

Your clients need a smooth and straightforward buying experience. Spell out who your products are for, how they work and the transformation they offer. When people don't have to guess, they can make decisions with ease.

## 6. Be visible

If you want clients to find you, you need to show up. Regular visibility builds trust and connection, which are essential for sales. The more you show up, the easier it gets.

## 7. Have a plan – and stick to it

Consistency is key. A simple, repeatable plan for sharing your key messages ensures your audience knows exactly what you offer and how it can help them. Avoid the temptation to constantly switch tactics – stick to your plan and give it time to work.

## The ten non-negotiables of selling well

### 8. Be yourself

Your audience buys into you as much as your products. Share pieces of your personality and let people connect with the real you. Authenticity builds trust and makes your business stand out.

### 9. Create content for every stage of the sales process

Your content should guide your audience through their decision-making journey. Post content intentionally, focusing on connection, confidence and clarity, rather than simply filling space on your social media feed.

### 10. Sell every day

People rarely buy the first time they see a product. Regularly share your offers and give your audience opportunities to engage with them. Consistent sales activity creates momentum and builds trust over time.

## Simplifying your sales

When you prioritize these needle-moving tasks, you can create a sales process that fits seamlessly into your daily routine. It's not about working harder or doing more – it's about working smarter and focusing on what truly drives results.

Sales is an energy game. By protecting your time and energy, and focusing on these non-negotiable tasks, you'll set yourself up for consistent growth without the risk of burn-out.

## So what? Over to you…

1. Practise talking about what you do – the more you do it, the easier it gets!

## The ten non-negotiables of selling well

2. Which of these 'non-negotiable' tasks do you feel most resistance towards? Why is that?

3. Commit to spending 30 minutes each day this week actioning one or more of these tasks. Where will you start?

# Day 5
# The buyer journey

In the early 2000s, I spent time studying consumer behaviour as part of my economics degree. Back then, it was widely believed that human decision-making was entirely logical – driven by carefully considered factors and predictable formulas. Yet, around the same time, a Harvard professor named Gerald Zaltman turned that notion on its head.

Zaltman's groundbreaking research revealed that 95% of purchasing decisions are in fact made subconsciously, driven by the part of the brain responsible for emotions.[2] People buy based on feelings first, and logic steps in afterward to validate the decision.

For us as business owners, this insight changes everything. If your sales efforts focus solely on logical features, you're missing the emotional connection that drives 95% of people to buy. Emotional resonance must come first – then details like features, pricing and other practical information can step in to support the decision.

## Selling is a journey, not a transaction

Selling is rarely a one-and-done moment. Your audience needs to connect with you emotionally before they even consider buying. If you've ever mentioned your product once and felt disheartened when it didn't sell immediately, know that this is normal. The sales process is about creating a journey that helps buyers move from 'I don't know you' to 'I trust you' and, eventually, to a confident decision.

## Who is your buyer?

Your buyer isn't just anyone. Your buyer is the person who is:

- Actively searching for what you sell
- Ready to take action now
- Equipped with the motivation and means to make the purchase

*The buyer journey*

Your job isn't to convince people to buy something they don't want – it's to stand out to those who genuinely need what you offer.

## The decision-maker's journey

The buyer journey is the path your potential clients take from discovering your business to deciding whether or not to purchase from you. This process consists of key phases:

1. **Awareness:** Potential clients need to know you exist.
2. **Emotional connection:** Once they've found you, they need to feel connected to you and your brand.
3. **Information gathering:** Buyers seek logical details to validate their emotions, such as how your product works and what results they can expect.
4. **Decision:** The buyer makes an informed choice, supported by both emotional and logical cues.

Your role is to make this journey as smooth and enjoyable as possible. Small businesses have a unique advantage here: you can use storytelling, human connection and authenticity to guide clients through this process.

## Why people buy

Zaltman's research showed that buying decisions are often rooted in the desire for improvement. People buy to:

- Solve a problem
- Gain something they desire
- Get better at doing or having something that feels difficult or inaccessible right now

By understanding what drives your audience – whether it's saving time, improving their confidence or achieving a specific result – you can position your products as solutions to their needs.

## Making it easy to buy

To help buyers make confident decisions, your content must guide them at every stage along the way. A consistent online presence that builds connection and provides clarity is essential. Most buyers research extensively before committing – 81% look online and 74% rely on social media to inform their decisions.[3]

Your job is to:

1. Show up consistently so your audience knows you're there.
2. Explain what your product does, who it's for and how it helps.
3. Provide resources that make decision-making easier, like frequently asked questions, testimonials or how-to guides.

The easier you make it for buyers to understand what your products do for them, the more sales you will make.

## Why 'no' is not a bad thing

It's important to remember that not every potential client will be the right fit for your business – and that's a good thing. Saying 'no' to clients who aren't a match protects your time, energy and reputation.

When your sales process is clear, your ideal clients will self-select, and those who aren't a fit will naturally opt out. This saves you from wasting time on unsuitable leads and ensures that the clients you do work with are aligned with your values and services.

*Sales Made Simple*

The buyer journey is about creating emotional connections and providing logical clarity to empower decision-making. By mapping out the steps you want your clients to take – from discovery to purchase – and creating content that supports each stage, you can make buying from you an easy and enjoyable experience. Next, we'll take a look at how you make yourself a perfect solution for clients...

### So what? Over to you...

1. Map out the journey you'd like your buyer to go on from first meet to final decision. What are the key steps?

## The buyer journey

2. What feeling do you want to thread through your buyer's experience with you? How can you ensure your content is connecting your buyer to that feeling at each stage of their journey?

3. How does your product bring your buyer closer to something they want? (E.g. saving them time, making/saving them money, helping them feel better about themselves/their relationships...)

## Day 6
# Solid sales foundations

As we saw in the Introduction, 60% of UK business owners don't use social media to promote their work and 90% feel invisible online.[4] Yet over 80% of purchasing decisions are influenced by online content.[5] The gap between buyer behaviour and small business visibility is staggering.

Arnold Schwarzenegger said that whatever your vocation, half the job is doing it and half the job is promoting it. And he's right. Whether you're an actor, an author or a furniture maker, the time you put into your craft is only ever half of the equation. If you want it to succeed, you must show up and talk about it. Consistently. So if right now you're spending more time on anything other than selling, it's time to rebalance things. Arnie didn't become one of the highest-grossing actors of all time by being the best actor – he did it by understanding the value of promoting his work.

The business owners thriving today are not the ones with the biggest budgets or largest audiences. They're the ones who know the value of talking about what they do to create sales opportunities.

## The foundations of selling well

Strong sales foundations rely on three areas of clarity: the product, the messaging and the promotion.

## The product

Your product must solve a specific problem for a specific audience. Many business owners struggle because their offer lacks focus. Be clear about:

- **Who it's for**: Identify the ideal buyer and their key challenges.
- **What it does**: Articulate the transformation your product delivers.
- **Why it matters**: Explain why your product makes life better – whether it saves time or money, or solves a pressing issue.

Instead of trying to appeal to everyone, specialize. A clearly defined niche helps your ideal client feel seen and understood. This specificity leads to easier sales because buyers can quickly self-identify with your offer.

## The messaging

Your message is how you communicate your product's value to potential clients. If your messaging is vague, unreliable or overly focused on you instead of them, it won't resonate. Shift the focus to your audience. They want to know:

- What's in it for them?
- How does this solve their problem?

For example:

| Vague message that focuses on creator | Clear message that focuses on client |
|---|---|
| 'I made this product to bring together my extensive research into UK motorways spanning 15 years.' | 'I made this product to stop you getting lost on car journeys.' |

| 'In this course, I share my skills as a writer.' | 'In this course I will teach you how to write your first novel, from approaching publishers to outlining the book structure and chapter dos and don'ts. You will learn everything you need to turn your idea into a finished book manuscript.' |
|---|---|

## The promotion

Even the best product with great messaging won't sell if no one sees it. That's where visibility comes in. Showing up consistently – whether on social media, through in-person networking or via a podcast or email newsletter – ensures your ideal clients know what's available and how to buy.

Promoting your work doesn't require hours of effort. It's about doing small, intentional actions daily to build connection and trust. The clearer you are, the easier it is for clients to find and buy from you.

## Get specific

Standing out isn't about shouting louder – it's about being specific. Each time someone asks you what you do, what they're really asking is 'What can you do for me?' A good rule of thumb is to follow the 'who, what, why' approach:

- **Who it's for:** Define your ideal client.
- **What it does:** Explain the problem you solve.
- **Why it matters:** Articulate the benefit for the client.

This enables the person you're talking with to see past your job title and get straight to considering whether you have something they need right now. In the few seconds you've got to make an impact, this maximizes the opportunity.

For example, let's say you're a wedding photographer. What are your favourite types of client or wedding? Maybe you're a wedding photographer for fun-loving couples who care more about the party than the traditional details. Perhaps your speciality is amazing dance floor shots. Maybe you focus on capturing the emotion of the day. Whatever your favourite aspects are, don't forget to tell people!

## Who is it for?

Are you for non-traditional couples? Dance floor-focused couples? Are country barn weddings your thing? Or something else?

## What does it do for them?

Do you deliver a beautiful, timeless set of photos that capture memories from the day that will last a lifetime? Is your focus is on capturing important family members throughout the day? Or is it that you know how to blend in easily with friends and family alike?

## Why should they care?

Are you good at relaxing camera-shy couples? Do you geek out over dance floor shots? Is your superpower gathering big groups and getting them in position at superspeed? Are you a winter wedding specialist who can take flattering photos even in low-light venues?

Whatever industry you work in, think about what makes you the right fit for a certain buyer and shift the way you talk so that the focus is more on them and what they stand to gain than it is on you and your expertise.

But before they can ask what you do, they have to find you, and that means getting visible...

*Solid sales foundations*

## Getting started with visibility

Visibility can feel daunting, but it's essential for growth. Here are five tips to make it easier, with thanks to visibility expert Vicki Knights:

1. **Reconnect with your purpose:** When fear of judgement creeps in, remember why you started your business. Focus on the people you want to help and the impact you want to make.
2. **Clarify your personal brand:** Get clear on your values, strengths and the unique style you bring to your work. Authenticity builds trust.
3. **Be yourself:** Showing up authentically is far more effective than trying to emulate others.
4. **Reframe visibility:** Think of it as sharing value, not self-promotion. You're helping potential clients solve a problem.
5. **Take small steps:** Whether it's posting a photo, sharing a story or pitching a podcast, every action builds confidence.

## Visibility is service

Being visible isn't about you – it's about helping your audience. If you aren't showing up, you're making it harder for potential clients to find the solution they're seeking. Whether you're posting online or networking in person, your message needs to answer:

- Who do you help?
- What problem do you solve?
- Why should they care?

The more you show up, the easier it gets. To make it even easier to get visible, why not think about getting some new headshots that make you feel really confident?

## *Solid sales foundations*

### ✏️ So what? Over to you...

1. When you think about who you want to buy your products, what are some of the exact things they are looking for help with?

2. How does your product make your clients' lives better? Does it achieve a specific goal? Will it save them time, evoke an emotion or something else?

## Solid sales foundations

3. Position your product as a specific and clear solution by completing the following sentence: 'I help [person] with [challenge] so that they can [achieve specific desired outcome].'

# Day 7
# Sales strategy step by step

Your sales strategy is your roadmap, helping you connect with the right clients in a clear, consistent and manageable way. A well-thought-out strategy eliminates random action, simplifies your process and ensures a high-quality client experience. Without a plan, it's easy to feel overwhelmed, take ineffective actions or fall into reactive sales – relying on word-of-mouth or referrals and hoping they come through. A proactive strategy, however, gives you control over your sales and lets you guide potential clients through a seamless process.

A robust sales strategy consists of four key stages: **Relevance**, **Audience Nurturing**, **Conversations** and **Experience**. These stages collectively make up the RACE framework for consistent sales.

## Relevance: building awareness

The first stage of the sales process is ensuring your products or services can be found by the right audience.

### Lead with clarity

Focus on the specific problem your client is looking to solve and how your product addresses it. Position your offering as the solution to a known need to create immediate clarity in your buyer's mind.

Key considerations:

1. **Who is your audience?** Be clear about who you're speaking to and what they want.
2. **What problem are they trying to solve?** Present your product as a solution to a specific problem.
3. **How does your product deliver on their needs?** Spell out the tangible benefits or transformations.

### Visibility is essential

Be where your clients are. Think strategically about the activities that will put you in front of your target audience. These might include networking, guest blogging, speaking on podcasts or collaborations with complementary businesses. Pair this visibility with messaging that highlights the relevance of your product.

Example activities:

- Attend networking events
- Write guest blog posts for sites your ideal clients frequent
- Collaborate with others who serve a similar audience

## Measuring relevance

You'll know this stage is working when you see your audience growing – whether that's through new followers, email signups or inquiries. If growth is stagnant, it's either because the right people aren't finding you or because your messaging isn't speaking directly to them and is failing to spark their curiosity.

## Audience nurturing: building emotional connection

The next step is to create an emotional connection that allows your audience to feel something. This is the stage where you nurture your audience by building connection and trust.

## Content to build emotion

Audience nurturing is about creating content that resonates with your potential clients and helps them feel something. Your goal is to move people from being curious (cold) to understanding the value of your offer (warm) to actively considering making a purchase (hot).

**Cold audience:** This group is new to your world. Focus on content that introduces your brand and highlights the problems you help solve. Connection-building content includes:

- Statistics or insights that frame the issue you address
- Personal stories about why you're passionate about solving this problem
- Introductory posts about your work and typical client results

**Warm audience:** These people already interact with your content. Now it's time to deepen their understanding of the results your product can deliver. Content for this stage includes:

- Explaining the transformation your product provides
- Highlighting who your product is designed for and why
- Sharing case studies or social proof

**Hot audience:** These clients are ready to make a decision. Focus on giving them the detailed information they need about the product experience and what they can expect if they buy. Your content should:

- Provide a clear breakdown of what's included
- Address common questions or concerns
- Offer calls to action to guide them toward the next step

## Measuring nurturing success

You'll know it's working when you start receiving enquiries, messages or questions about your offers. If this isn't happening, it may be a sign that your messaging isn't focused enough on creating a feeling or that it needs to relate more specifically to the feelings of your ideal buyer.

## Conversations: establishing suitability

One of the most valuable things you can do for your client is to have conversations that help them decide if your product is right for them. This stage is about providing tailored service and showcasing your integrity, not hard selling.

### Sales conversations with integrity

A great sales conversation is about understanding your potential client's needs, assessing whether your product is a good fit and allowing the buyer to feel able to make informed decisions in a timely manner. A helpful framework for these conversations includes:

1. **Introduction:** Understand what they are looking to achieve.
2. **Research:** Ask questions to uncover their specific challenges and goals.
3. **Qualification:** Determine if your product is truly the right fit. If it is, explain why it is; and if it isn't, be honest!
4. **Invitation:** Once you've established whether you can help, make recommendations about the best route forward.

Sales calls are a brilliant opportunity to show your potential client your focus is on establishing suitability for them. Lead with curiosity, not assumptions. Your role is to provide information, answer questions and help the client feel confident in their decision.

## Saying no

Not every conversation will lead to a sale, and that's a good thing. If your product isn't the right fit, or if red flags emerge during the conversation, it's better to say no. This ensures you're working with the clients who'll benefit most from your products, protects your energy, and minimizes the risk of dissatisfaction down the line.

## Experience: delivering excellence

The final stage of the sales process builds even more momentum around providing an exceptional client experience. This not only helps you retain clients and encourage repeat purchases, but also turns happy clients into brand advocates who will become your biggest champions and recommend you far and wide.

## Why experience matters

A high-quality sales experience is one of the most powerful sales tools you have. It makes your business stand out and can have a significant impact on your reputation. It increases the likelihood of:

- Repeat business
- Positive reviews and referrals
- Higher perceived value, allowing you to charge premium prices

## Designing a memorable experience

Think about how you want clients to feel throughout their journey with you. From their first interaction to the post-purchase follow-up, every touchpoint is an opportunity to demonstrate your commitment to excellence. Ask yourself:

- What impression do you want clients to have of your business?
- Are there opportunities to make their experience more seamless or enjoyable?
- How can you communicate your dedication to quality at every stage?

## Building your RACE sales strategy

A great sales strategy focuses on all four stages so that buyers have a productive journey to easeful decisions and you make more sales. Each stage supports the next:

- **Relevance** brings the right people into your world.
- **Audience nurturing** helps them connect with your business and build trust.
- **Conversations** ensure they're making informed decisions.
- **Experience** delivers value and creates lasting loyalty.

Follow these steps to create a clear, repeatable process, simplify your sales action and elevate the client experience long before they pay you. With this plan in place, you'll know exactly what to focus on and can grow your business with confidence.

## So what? Over to you...

1. Brainstorm 2–3 actions for each RACE stage.

2. Looking at the list you just made, which actions feel most aligned and energizing to you? Prioritize these actions.

3. Are there any stages that feel more challenging than others? Why might this be, and how can you support yourself through this so that you feel more at ease?

# Day 8
# The power of your personal brand

Your personal brand is a brilliant tool for creating sales opportunities naturally. It's more than just your skill set – it's the way you show up in the world, the values you hold and the story you tell. A strong personal brand allows people to connect with you on a human level, which speeds up the sales process and builds lasting relationships.

By stepping into your personal brand and letting people get to know the person behind the business, you can stop playing small and start creating more meaningful impact in your field.

*The power of your personal brand*

## What is a personal brand?

Your personal brand is the story you tell about who you are and what you stand for, outside of the literal products or services you sell. It's how you connect with your audience on a deeper level. People don't just buy products – they buy relationships, trust and shared experiences.

Connection takes time to build. Most people won't buy the first time they come across your business. They want to get to know you first. Through consistent, meaningful content, you can build the trust that eventually leads to sales.

Your personal brand gives your business context and makes it easier for people to understand why you do what you do. It's the story that helps potential clients see the value in your work and makes them feel they are buying from someone they can trust.

## Sharing your story

To build a strong personal brand, you need to be visible, genuine and clear about what makes you unique. Here's how to start:

1. **Share your point of view**
   What makes your perspective unique? You don't need to reinvent the wheel – simply sharing your stance on common problems or trends in your industry can help you stand out. Your audience will connect with your distinct approach to solving their challenges.

2. **Find the sweet spot**
   Your personal brand lies at the intersection of what drives you personally and what your audience relates to. By identifying where these overlap, you can create content that feels authentic while resonating deeply with your audience. Think about these questions:
   - What values or experiences do you want to share?
   - What is your unique take on issues in your field?
   - How does your work create change or improvement?

3. **Tell your story**
   Sharing defining moments in your journey helps your audience connect with you on a personal level. What experiences have shaped your values, your work and your approach?

*The power of your personal brand*

Sharing these can create common ground and build trust.

4. **Be genuine and authentic**
   Authenticity is key to a successful personal brand. People can sense when you're trying to be someone you're not, and it undermines trust. Instead, lean into your natural tone of voice and share the parts of your story that truly matter to you.

5. **Showcase your expertise**
   Let your audience see your knowledge and skills in action. Share content that demonstrates how you can help them, and let your personality shine through in the process.

## Why your personal brand matters

A strong personal brand has numerous benefits for your business:

- **Faster and deeper connections:** A personal brand helps you share your story to enable clients to feel connected to you, speeding up their decision-making process.

- **Future-proofing:** A personal brand allows you to pivot, evolve and explore new opportunities without losing your audience.
- **Increased sales:** People are more likely to buy from you if you are someone they feel they know and trust. Even if your audience is small, your personal brand can help you increase sales.
- **Differentiation:** A personal brand makes you stand out from competitors in a crowded marketplace.
- **Reputation protection:** A strong personal brand builds trust and credibility, protecting you from comparison and criticism.

## Selling through connection

The more you share of yourself – your opinions, your journey, your values – the stronger the connection you build with your audience. And as we've seen, connection drives sales. People are more likely to buy when they feel they know, like and trust the person behind the business.

Here are the key elements of an effective personal brand:

- **Stories:** Share the experiences that shaped your business.

## *The power of your personal brand*

- **Values:** Let your audience know what matters most to you.
- **Personality:** Show up as yourself – quirks and all.
- **Expertise:** Position yourself as the go-to person for your niche.

By weaving these elements into your content, you create a personal brand that feels authentic, relatable and compelling.

## Future-proofing your business

A strong personal brand isn't just about what you're selling today – it's about building a platform for future opportunities. By establishing yourself as a trusted voice in your field, you create a foundation that allows you to evolve, pivot or expand into new areas without losing your audience's trust or interest.

## Increased sales

Your personal brand doesn't just help you connect with people – it directly impacts your sales. People are far more likely to buy from someone they feel they know and trust, even if your audience is small. The key lies in showcasing your human side.

When your audience sees the person behind the business – your values, your story, your perspective – they feel better connected to you. This connection removes hesitation, making the sales process smoother and faster. It's not just about showcasing what you sell, but about helping your clients feel they're buying from someone who genuinely understands their needs.

As small business owners, this is our advantage over larger, faceless companies. Use it! Show up consistently, share your expertise and be authentic. The more you connect with your audience, the more confident they'll feel in choosing your products and services.

## Differentiation

In crowded markets, standing out can sometimes feel impossible. Your personal brand is the antidote to being unseen. Use it to set yourself apart from competitors.

What makes your perspective or approach different? Maybe it's a specific value you hold, a niche insight or a unique experience that shapes the way you work. Sharing these elements gives your audience a reason to choose you over others, not just because of your skills but because of who you are and what you represent.

Differentiation isn't about being radically different – it's about being unmistakably you. When your audience sees you as someone they align with on a deeper level, you stop competing and start creating your own space in the market.

## Reputation protection

A strong personal brand protects your reputation in ways that go far beyond damage control. By consistently showing up, sharing your values and delivering excellent service, you create a foundation of trust and credibility that helps shield you from comparison or criticism.

People are less likely to question your skills or intentions when they've already seen your integrity and passion in action. When challenges arise – whether it's a dissatisfied client, a tough review or just the nature of doing business – your established personal brand provides context and trust. It assures your audience that you're someone who handles issues with grace and care.

Additionally, a strong personal brand prevents you from being seen as interchangeable with competitors.

You become more than your skill set or product – you become the go-to person for your audience because of the connection you've built over time.

These benefits – combined with faster connections and future-proofing – show just how powerful a personal brand can be. By investing in building your story and showing up authentically, you're creating a foundation for long-term success.

### So what? Over to you...

1. How would you summarize the values you are led by in three words? Are these core values expressed clearly on your website or in the content you create?

2. Do you have a unique observation to share about your area of expertise? Do you see the world differently to others in your industry or niche? How?

3. What have been the defining points in your journey that have led you to where you are today? What stands out to you that may resonate with the journey your audience is on?

# Day 9
# Turning your content into sales

Social media is a ready-made sales machine for business owners who know how to utilise it. It allows you access to the people who are ready to buy from you, who are online every day of the year. All you have to know is how to use it to create sales – which is exactly what I'm showing you in this chapter.

The most important step is to get started. The second most important step is to keep going! The content you post on social media will tell your audience everything they need to know, if you let it.

## The magic of social media

Social media works as an ideal sales tool because:

1. It builds **connection** by helping your audience get to know you.
2. It builds **confidence** in your expertise and ability to deliver results.
3. It delivers **conviction**, giving your audience the certainty they need to make a purchase.

## Selling on social media: why it's worth your time

Your ideal clients are already there, 365 days a year, 7 days a week, 24 hours a day. Consider this: 84% of the UK population uses social media,[6] with platforms like Instagram and Facebook dominating.

For small business owners, this provides an incredible and highly lucrative opportunity to blend service, human connection and problem-solving to attract buyers. Most importantly, social media allows you to scale the personal connection your clients crave, all while being strategic with your time.

## How to use social media strategically

Choose the platform that best suits your business goals, audience and personality. Here's how to leverage it effectively...

## Decide what social media will do for your business

Social media can serve different purposes in your sales process:

- **Visibility:** Attract new clients and raise awareness.
- **Engagement:** Nurture relationships and deepen connections with your audience.
- **Sales:** Provide clear pathways for your audience to purchase.

Be clear about how social media supports your sales plan. Are you using it for all stages of the sales process or just one?

## Choose the right platform

Not every platform will suit your business. Here's a quick overview of major platforms:

- **Instagram:** Great for sharing a mix of videos, photos and written content.
- **Facebook:** Ideal for building communities through pages or groups.
- **TikTok:** Best for engaging video content and younger audiences.
- **LinkedIn:** Perfect for professional networking and thought leadership.
- **Pinterest:** A visual search engine for inspiration and productivity.
- **YouTube:** Ideal for in-depth educational content.

Pick the platform your target buyers use the most, and use a format that aligns with your strengths.

## The three types of content that drive sales

Creating content for social media doesn't have to be overwhelming. Instead of posting random updates, focus on three types of sales-focused content: connection content, confidence content and conviction content.

*Turning your content into sales*

## 1. Connection content

This is designed to welcome new people into your world. It's the first step in helping your audience get to know you. Think of it as the 'handshake' of your social media presence.

Examples of connection content include:

- Stories about your personal journey
- Behind-the-scenes glimpses of your work process
- Posts that highlight shared values or interests

Connection content helps people who are new to your brand feel an emotional connection, making them curious to learn more.

## 2. Confidence content

This content builds trust and deepens your audience's understanding of your expertise. It's about demonstrating that you know your stuff and can deliver results.

Examples of confidence content include:

- Sharing success stories or testimonials from previous clients

- Providing tips, insights or quick how-tos related to your niche
- Highlighting common problems your audience faces and how you solve them

Confidence content reassures your audience that they're in capable hands

## 3. Conviction content

Conviction content enables sales to happen more easily. This content shows your audience why they should buy from you and makes it easy for them to take the next step.

Examples of conviction content include:

- Tell people who your product is for/is not for
- Posts explaining what your product does, who it's for and the results it delivers
- Answers to frequently asked questions or responses to common objections

Without conviction content, even the most loyal followers may not convert into buyers.

## Avoiding filler content

Not all content is created equal. Avoid 'filler' posts that don't serve a purpose, such as:

- Inspirational quotes unrelated to your brand
- Random updates with no relevance to your audience's needs
- Vague mentions of your product without context

Instead, focus on the sales content that moves your audience along their decision-making journey.

## Crafting a balanced content strategy

For social media to truly support your sales process, your content needs to balance:

- **Cold content** (connection): attracts new people and sparks interest
- **Warm content** (confidence): nurtures trust and builds familiarity
- **Hot content** (conviction): activates decision-making and leads to sales

Create a schedule to ensure you're consistently producing content for each stage. For example, you might decide to post two pieces of connection content, two pieces of confidence content and one piece of conviction content each week.

## Final thoughts

Social media is a powerful tool for small business owners, but it works best when used with specific sales intention. By creating content that supports each stage of your audience's decision-making process, you ensure your time spent online translates directly into sales.

Let's recap the key points:

- Use social media strategically to support your overall sales plan.
- Choose a platform that aligns with your goals and audience.
- Focus on connection, confidence and conviction content to drive meaningful engagement and sales.

In the final chapter, you'll get a 30-day content challenge to help you put these strategies into action and start turning your followers into buyers. Let's go!

*Turning your content into sales*

### ✎ So what? Over to you...

1. Look back at Day 7 and the sales plan you made: which stages do you want social media to support you with?

2. Decide how many pieces of content you will create each week (be realistic!), and plan how you will stay consistent.

*Turning your content into sales*

3. Block out the time in your calendar *now* to create content. How will you use your first session?

# Day 10
# Take the 30-day sales challenge

This 30-day challenge is designed to help you focus on taking the right action daily, showing up in a few minutes a day and building sales momentum fast. By following the prompts provided, you'll create content that speaks to audiences at every stage of the buying process: cold (connection), warm (confidence), and hot (conviction). This approach simplifies sales activity, turning social media into a tool for consistent, effective selling – one post at a time.

## Why a 30-day challenge?

Daily sales activity keeps your audience engaged, nurtured and informed. Whether you're introducing your business to potential clients, building trust or encouraging conversions, if you want more sales, this is how you do it.

The goal isn't perfection but progress. It's about committing to consistent action – just a few minutes each day – to create a habit that generates long-term results. By cycling through the prompts, you'll find your voice, grow more confident in self-promotion and create momentum that feeds your business.

## Everyday selling benefits

Selling every day means your audience is always informed and ready to buy on their own timeline. Benefits of taking a few minutes a day to prioritize your sales activity include:

- More confidence in your promotion
- Improved communication in what your offer provides
- Better results in less time
- Momentum that creates a snowball effect in your sales
- Easier sales experience for clients
- Faster progression to decision
- Consistency beyond measure

- Social media use that bolsters your sales instead of stealing your time
- More sales in the small business economy
- More confidence in talking about what you do
- No need to do 'big pitches' ever again (unless you want to!)

When you master everyday selling, you will always be able to make money, bring ideal clients into your business and spend your time doing work you love.

## How it works

- **Who is this for?** Anyone who wants to simplify their sales strategy, get visible and build traction without overwhelm.
- **What's the process?** Each day, pick a prompt tailored to your audience's stage in the buying journey (cold, warm or hot) and create a short, clear piece of content based on it.
- **How long will it take?** Around 30 minutes a day. This is not about overthinking – just focusing on regular, repeatable actions.

*Take the 30-day sales challenge*

# Content prompts for the buying journey

## 1. For cold audiences: connection content

Cold audiences are new to your world and don't yet know why they should stick around. Connection content builds curiosity, introduces your expertise and connects their aspirations with your solutions. It shows your audience why they should pay attention and follow you.

### Ten prompts for building connection

1. Introduce yourself and share what you do.
2. Explain why your business exists and the problems you solve.
3. Share a personal experience that led you to work in your industry.
4. Use a relevant statistic to highlight the problem your audience faces.
5. Create intrigue about your product by sharing its main applications.
6. Relate key parts of your journey to your audience's struggles.
7. Address a pain point with actionable advice (e.g. 'Three tools to stop X').

8. Offer a tip tied to an aspiration (e.g. 'Want to achieve X? Here's how.').
9. Describe a common struggle you've helped clients overcome.
10. Share a case study that illustrates a client's transformation.

## 2. For warm audiences: confidence content

Warm audiences are familiar with you but need reassurance to move forward. Confidence content deepens trust and nurtures the connection by showing how you solve problems and the results you deliver.

### Ten prompts for building confidence

1. Describe what clients can expect when working with you.
2. Explain a common mistake your audience makes and how to avoid it.
3. Discuss why people often get stuck and how to move past it.
4. Highlight how you simplify challenges for your clients.

*Take the 30-day sales challenge*

5. Share when it's the right time to work with someone like you.
6. Clarify who your products are (and aren't) for.
7. Share what's missing in your industry that you aim to provide.
8. Explain the results clients can expect from working with you.
9. Reveal what drives you to do this work and what fuels your passion.
10. Discuss your beliefs or philosophy around your subject matter.

## 3. For hot audiences: conviction content

Hot audiences are ready to take action but need clarity and assurance. Conviction content removes any remaining doubts by clearly explaining the transformation you offer and inviting them to make a decision.

### Ten prompts for building conviction

1. Explain who your products are for (and who they aren't).

2. Describe your process and how it transitions clients from A to B.
3. Highlight the transformation clients can expect after working with you.
4. Share testimonials or case studies showing real client results.
5. Post screenshots of positive client feedback or go live with a happy client.
6. Explain what clients will experience when working with you, step by step.
7. Clarify what clients will and won't get from your offer.
8. Highlight tangible (e.g. calls, resources) and intangible (e.g. confidence) benefits.
9. Help clients self-identify when it's the right time to buy.
10. Address common objections and ease worries (e.g. time, cost or results).

## Bonus tip: play sales bingo!

For added variety, turn the prompts into a bingo game. You can download your sales bingo sheet with 30 prompts on it from my website: saradalrymple.co.uk/moresalesplease. Challenge yourself to complete all 30 prompts in a month – or mix and match them depending on your focus.

## What to do when it's working: selling in direct messages

As your sales activity gains momentum, you'll notice more enquiries coming in. This is an opportunity to provide stellar service and guide potential clients with clarity and care, so let's talk through best practice.

### Top tips for direct messaging sales conversations

- **Be confident:** Remember, clients often message before buying. Approach these conversations with confidence and clarity about your process.
- **Ask questions:** Open the loop by asking what brought them to you. This helps you uncover their needs.
- **Diagnose first:** Understand the root problem before offering a solution.
- **Assess suitability:** Only recommend your offer if it's the right fit. Be honest – your integrity matters.

- **Follow through:** Deliver on your promises to create happy clients who refer you to others.

## Why selling every day works

Social media lets you share bite-sized, meaningful content that nurtures your audience and supports sales. By showing up daily with clear, valuable messages, you build trust, keep your audience engaged and encourage decision-making. Make it a completely normal part of your day, not an occasional occurrence.

Take the 30-day challenge and you'll not only grow your business but also develop a sustainable, effective sales routine that you can rely on long-term. Remember, it's not about perfection – it's about action!

## Top tips for the challenge

- Start wherever you are. If you're brand new to posting, aim to start a new habit. If you're currently posting twice a week, can you increase this to three? If you're already posting 10 times a month, can you challenge yourself to increase this to 20? This is all about taking

## Take the 30-day sales challenge

action as many days in the month as you can without feeling overwhelmed.
- Progress over perfection! The aim is to get into the swing of taking daily action in a few minutes a day. It's not about being perfect – it's about getting into the habit of showing up and giving your audience a regular opportunity to get to know what's available.
- Set aside 30 minutes each day maximum to do your sales activity. Block the time out in your calendar so it actually happens!

## So what? Over to you…

1. That's easy – take the challenge!

# Conclusion

There's a saying in the small business community that goes something along the lines of 'every time you buy from a small business owner, they do a little happy dance'. I love a happy dance, and if it's to a nineties tune, even better!

Hearing your phone or computer 'ping' with a sale coming through never fails to raise a smile. Getting paid for work you love to create by people who value the way you do what you do is a whole vibe, and it just never gets old. But that ping of a sale is about so much more than dancing. Financial independence, effecting change, growing the economy without selling your soul... the list goes on and on. The small business community is such an important part of the UK economy, and the more it thrives, the better for everyone!

You now have the foundation, the method and the prompts to equip you to do your daily promotional activity with confidence. Chapter by chapter, we have explored how to increase your sales in less time so that you can grow without the grind.

*Sales Made Simple*

Far from the general perception that it's 'hard' to make money or to sell well, making lots and lots of sales for your business gets to be easy when you have a plan that's aligned for you. Now that you've read this book, you have everything you need to do just that and to do it in a way that fits into your daily life in just a few minutes. Through repeatable action, you can start and keep going, even when life gets in the way, without having to rely on inspiration, motivation or luck.

I truly believe that sales skills are the best gift you can give your business. They allow you to sustain your business, make money on your own terms and do work you love for as long as you want to.

Einstein said, 'Life is like riding a bicycle. To keep your balance, you must keep moving.' The same is true with sales. Your 30-day challenge awaits, and the more you do it, the better your results will be. Eventually, promoting your products will be so natural you won't need the prompts any more, but until then, use them as much as you need.

Small and medium-sized enterprises already contribute more than half of private sector turnover in the UK, and that's without 60% of them harnessing the power of confident promotion online. Half of business owners polled by OnePoll feel they

## Conclusion

could have made more sales if they had marketed themselves properly online.

Imagine the additional revenue, the jobs and the impact that would be generated from people doing what they love and talking about it more regularly on the internet. As I always say, if all of the business owners using social media spent just a few minutes each day promoting and selling their products, the amount of income created would be mind-blowing.

Let's blow some minds and do some happy dances, shall we?

Sara x

https://saradalrymple.co.uk/

# Endnotes

[1] Holly & Co. Available from https://holly.co/campaign-shop-independent-2023/

[2] G. Zaltman, *How Customers Think: Essential insights into the mind of the market* (2003).

[3] Yaqub M., *26+ powerful small business marketing statistics for 2024*, Business Dasher. Available from www.businessdit.com/small-business-online-marketing-statistics/

[4] Holly & Co.

[5] Yaqub M., *26+ powerful small business marketing statistics for 2024*.

[6] Yaqub M., *26+ powerful small business marketing statistics for 2024*.

# Enjoyed this?
# Then you'll love…

*More Sales Please: Promote your small business online, make consistent sales, grow without the grind* by Sara Nasser Dalrymple

'The ultimate companion for any small business owner' – Holly Tucker, Founder of notonthehighstreet and Holly & Co

'I dare you to read this book and NOT make more sales – you couldn't have a better guide!' – Lucy Sheridan, The Comparison Coach

'Filled with straightforward advice that will help your business grow' – Emma Jones, Founder of Enterprise Nation

Have you ever:

- Told yourself you're not a natural salesperson?
- Procrastinated on promoting your business because it feels awkward?

- Launched something new, only to be met with deafening silence?

If you answered yes to any of these, then *More Sales Please* is for you! Most business owners have never been taught how to promote what they do with ease – until now. Say goodbye to guesswork and discover the step-by-step process to effortless sales in just 30 minutes a day.

Sara Nasser Dalrymple is a business mentor, strategist and educator and the go-to sales expert in the small business community. Based on 20 years of sales and marketing experience, her simple, actionable advice has helped hundreds of business owners transform the way they feel about selling and achieve long-lasting success through confident, sleaze-free self-promotion.

# Other 6-Minute Smarts titles

*Building Great Teams* (based on *Workshop Culture* by Alison Coward)

*Do Change Better* (based on *How to be a Change Superhero* by Lucinda Carney)

*How to be Happy at Work* (based on *My Job Isn't Working!* by Michael Brown)

*How to Get to Know Your Customer* (based on *Do Penguins Eat Peaches?* by Katie Tucker)

*The Listening Leader* (based on *The Listening Shift* by Janie van Hool)

*Mastering People Management* (based on *Mission: To Manage* by Marianne Page)

*No-Nonsense PR* (based on *Hype Yourself* by Lucy Werner)

*Present Like a Pro* (based on *Executive Presentations* by Jacqui Harper)

*Reimagine Your Career* (based on *Work/Life Flywheel* by Ollie Henderson)

*The Speed Storytelling Toolkit* (based on *Exposure* by Felicity Cowie)

*Write to Think* (based on *Exploratory Writing* by Alison Jones)

Look out for more titles coming soon! Visit www.practicalinspiration.com for all our latest titles.